LAOCOON

Head of Laocoon.

LAOCOON

The Influence of the Group
Since its Rediscovery

by Margarete Bieber

Revised and Enlarged Edition

With Photographs by Ernest Nash
Fototeca Unione Roma
and Archivio Fotografico Gallerie
Musei Vaticani

Wayne State University Press, Detroit, 1967

Preface

This little book is the result of the convergence of different studies: the investigation of the character of the late Hellenistic sculpture; the study of the relationship of three great classical writers, Winckelmann, Lessing, and Goethe, to ancient art; the consideration of the best way to illustrate lectures on ancient art. I found answers to all three problems in the Laocoon group as described and used for the demonstration of artistic, chronological, historical, ethical, moral, literary, and philosophical ideas by authors from Pliny to modern writers and also in the new type of detail photographs by Ernest Nash.

I believe that there is a need for small books to illustrate single important works of art with pictures and discussions from all possible angles, in order to introduce students and laymen to the spirit of special periods of art and to lead them to historical knowledge as well as to art appreciation.

I wish to thank Professor Erwin Panofsky, of Princeton, the Institute of Advanced Studies, for his good advice to include the effect of the Laocoon on the artists of the sixteenth and seventeenth centuries in this study.

MARGARETE BIEBER

NEW YORK
JANUARY 3, 1942

Preface

To the Revised and Enlarged Edition

A new edition of this little book is justified, for the Laocoon group is again an object of lively discussions. While it is still unique, related Homeric groups by the same three artists have been found in a cave at Sperlonga, part of a palace of the emperor Tiberius: Filippo Magi has taken the Laocoon apart and has attained a quite different and convincing reconstruction with the help of new discoveries. The generally accepted date has been challenged by Gisela Richter and Magi.

I wish to thank Professor Bernard Goldman of Wayne State University for encouraging me to make this revised edition.

NEW YORK, CHRISTMAS, 1966.

Illustrations and Sources

11. Drawing by Rubens, Back of Laocoon. *Master Drawings* II, 2, Fig. 8.

12. Drawing by Rubens, the Younger Son. *Master Drawings* II, 2, Fig. 9.

13. Front View of Head of Laocoon. *Phot. Archivio, Gallerie e Musei Vaticane X.6.16.*

14. Head of Laocoon, three quarter view. *Phot. Nash, Fototeca Unione Rome 44010.*

15. Right Arm of Laocoon by Michelangelo. *Phot. Nash, Fototeca Unione Rome 4429.*

16. Right Arm of Laocoon, found by Pollak, now used for the Group. *Phot. Vatican XXXII, 120-55.*

17. Reconstruction of the Group in Dresden. *Cast. Phot. German Archaeological Institute, Rome, 66.2508.*

18. Death of Laocoon and his Sons, Wallpainting in Casa di Menandro, Pompeii. *Phot. Nash, Fototeca Unione 4727.*

19. Group of Laocoon and his Sons, reconstructed by Magi. *Phot. Vat.*

20. Group of Laocoon and his Sons, restored by Magi. *Phot. Vat.*

21. Younger Son of Laocoon. *Phot. Nash, Fototeca Unione 4421.*

22. Elder Son of Laocoon. *Phot. Nash, Fototeca Unione 4419.*

23. Upper Part of the Group. *Phot. Nash, Fototeca Unione 4416.*

24. Lower Part of the Group. *Phot. Nash, Fototeca Unione 4417.*

25. Lower Part of the Elder Son. *Phot. Nash, Fototeca Unione 4414.*

26. Upper Part of the Elder Son. *Phot. Nash, Fototeca Unione 4423.*

27. Upper Part of the Younger Son. *Phot. Nash, Fototeca Unione 12113.*

The Laocoon group in the Belvedere of the Vatican (Figure 1)[1] is probably the most widely discussed work of sculpture which we possess from antiquity. The oldest of its descriptions which have come down to us is the following passage from Pliny's *Natural History* XXXVI. 37.

"There are many whose fame is not preserved. In some cases the glory of the finest works is obscured by the number of the artists, since no one of them can monopolize the credit, nor can the names of more than one be handed down. This is the case with the Laocoon, which stands in the palace of the Emperor Titus, a work to be preferred to all that the arts of painting and sculpture have produced. Out of one block of stone the consummate artists, Hagesandros, Polydoros, and

[1] Walter Amelung, *Skulpturen des Vatikanischen Museums*, II (1908), 181 ff., Cortile del Belvedere, No. 74, Pl. 20. To the Bibliography on pp. 202–5 must be added: Guy Dickens, *Hellenistic Sculpture* (1920), pp. 1, 50 f.; A. W. Lawrence, *Later Greek Sculpture* (1927), pp. 40, 130, Pl. 67; Gisela Richter, *Sculpture and Sculptors of the Greeks* (1930), pp. 50, 82, 297 f., Figs. 225, 763–64. Idem, *Three Critical Periods in Greek Sculpture* (1951), 49, 66–70, Figs. 66, 68. M. Bieber, *The Sculpture of the Hellenistic Age* (1961), 134 f., Figs. 530–531. W. Helbig, *Führer durch die Sammlungen Klassischer Altertümer* in Rom, Fourth ed. fully revised by Hermine Speier et al. I (1963), 102–166, no. 219 (Werner Fuchs). Hellmut Sichtermann, *Laokoon* (Opus Nobila 3, 1957). Idem, *Laokoon*, "Einführung." Reclam, Stuttgart (1964).

Athenodoros of Rhodes made, after careful planning, Laocoon, his sons, and the snakes marvelously entwined about them."

When the statue came to light again on January 14, 1506, artists, poets, and scholars were unanimous in their praise and enthusiasm. The statue was at once identified as the one described by Pliny, as is shown in a letter by Cesare Trivulzio, dated June, 1506:[2] "The first artists of the period, Michelangelo and Giovanni Cristofano Romano, deny, however, that Pliny's statement saying that the three figures are carved out of one piece of marble is right, for they found about four joints. . . . All, however, are of the opinion that the statues are most excellent and deserving of every praise." Several poets honored the statue at once with poems, among which the one by the learned Jacopo Sadoleto (1477–1547) is considered by Trivulzio "as having described the Laocoon and his sons no less elegantly with his pen than the artists have done it with the chisel." The poem expresses the conception which the late Renaissance and early Baroque period had of the Laocoon. They saw it as an example of extreme naturalism and unrestrained emotion, that is, ideals which are in accordance with the conceptions of the then contemporary art. It gives the best idea of the meaning which the group had for the sixteenth and also for the following two centuries, as even Lessing has inserted it in his *Loakoon*.[3]

[2] The names are incorrectly given as "Giovannangelo Romano" and "Michel Cristofano Fiorentino" in Giovanni G. Bottari, *Raccolta di lettere sulla pittura, scultura ed architettura*, III (1759), 321 f., No. 196; *Raccolta di lettere*, III (1822), 474; Bottari and Ticozzi, *Lettere pittoriche*, III, 475. For the finding of the statue in the "House of Titus," on the Esquiline, near the so-called Sette Sale, see Carlo Fea, *Miscellanea philologica*, I (1790), 329. For the enthusiasm after the discovery, see F. de Mély, "La Tête de Laocoon," in *Monuments Piot*, XVI (1909), 210 ff.

[3] Gotthold Ephraim Lessing, *Laokoon*, appeared 1766. Translation by Wilkinson in A. Hamann and L. E. Upcott, *Laokoon* (Oxford, 1892), pp. 57 f., 242 f. The poem is also in *Poemata selecta Italorum* (Oxford, 1808).

The Poem of Jacobus Sadoletus
on the Statue of Laocoon

Translated by H. S. Wilkinson

From heaped-up mound of earth and from the heart
Of mighty ruins, lo! long time once more
Has brought Laocoon home, who stood of old
In princely palaces and graced thy halls,
Imperial Titus. Wrought by skill divine
(Even learned ancients saw no nobler work),
The statue now from darkness saved returns
To see the stronghold of Rome's second life.
What shall begin and what shall end my lay?
The hapless father and his children twain?
The snakes of aspect dire in winding coils?
The serpents' ire, their knotted tails, their bites?
The anguish, real, though but marble, dies?
The mind recoils and pity's self appalled,
Gazing on voiceless statues beats her breast.
Two serpents flushed with rage gather in coils
To one loose ring, and glide in winding orbs,
And wrap three bodies in their twisted chain.
Scarce can the eyes endure to look upon
The dreadful death, the cruel tragedy.
One serpent darting at Laocoon's self,
Enraps him all, above, below; then strikes
With poisonous bite his side; the body shrinks
From such embrace. Behold the writhing limbs,
The side that starts recoiling from the wound.
By keen pain goaded and the serpent's bite,
Laocoon groans, and struggling from his side
To pluck the cruel teeth, in agony
His left hand grapples with the serpent's neck.
The sinews tighten, and the gathered strength

13

Of all his body strains his arm in vain;
Poison overcomes him; wounded sore he groans.
The other serpent now with sudden glide
Returned, darts under him its shiny length,
Entwines his knees below and binds him fast.
The knees press outward, and the leg compressed
By tightening windings swells; the blood confined
Chokes up the vitals and swells black the veins.
His sons no less the same wild strength attacks,
And strangles them with swift embrace and tears
Their little limbs; even now the gory breast
Of one whose dying voice his father calls
Has been its pasture; round him wrap its coils
And crush him in the mighty winding folds.
The other boy, unhurt, unbitten yet,
Uplifts his foot to unloose the serpent's tail;
His father's anguish seen he stands aghast,
Transfixed with horror—his loud wailings stay,
His falling teardrops stay—in double dread.

Then ye, the makers of so great a work,
Great workmen, still in lasting fame renowned
(Although by better deeds a deathless name
Is sought, although to some it was given to leave
A higher talent far to coming glory).
It is noble still to seize what chance is given
For praise, and strive the highest peak to gain.
It is yours with living shapes to quicken stone,
To give hard marble feeling till it breathes.
We gaze upon the passion, anger, pain,
We all but hear the groans, so great your skill,
You famous Rhodes of old extolled. Long time
The graces of your art lay low; again
Rome sees them in a new day's kindly light,

She honours them with many a looker on,
And on the ancient work new charms are shed.
Then better far by talent or by toil
To increase the span of fate, than still increase
Or pride or wealth or empty luxury.

Besides this at the same time learned and poetical reflection, the most fruitful soil for effect of the Laocoon was art. The artists of the late Renaissance and Baroque found emotional and formal inspiration in this artistically and technically so accomplished late Greek work.[4] Perhaps the earliest engraving is the one by Marco Dente (Figure 2), a pupil of Marc Antonio Raimondi, born in Ravenna, who lived later in Rome, where he died in 1527.[5] He gave a fine and faithful rendering of the not yet restored group. Later he added to this a Baroque variation of the subject in a wide landscape (Figure 3).[6] Laocoon throws up both arms in a gesture of

[4] See Marcel Brion, *Michel-Ange* (1940), pp. 158 ff.; translated from the French by James Whitall: "The discovery of the Laocoon was to be an important date in the history of European art."

[5] Fig. 2, the engraving by Marco Dente, is described in Johann David Passavant, *Le Peintre-Graveur*, I (1860), 70, No. 48, and in Adam von Bartsch, *Le Peintre Graveur*, XIV (1867), 268 f., No. 353. See also Fritz Wichert, *Darstellung und Wirklichkeit*, p. 21, No. 40, Pl. IX. P. Kristeller, in Thieme and Becker, *Künstler-Lexikon*, IX, 82. Henry Thode, *Die Antiken in den Stichen Marcantons, Agostino Veneziano und Marco Dentes* (1881), frontispiece (Pl. 1), pp. 13 ff., No. 35. The impression from which Fig. 2 was taken is in Antonio Lafreri, *Speculum Romanae magnificentiae*, Vol. II, folio 45. This recent acquisition to the Department of Prints of the Metropolitan Museum was kindly brought to my attention by Mr. William M. Ivins, Jr., the Curator. The Lafreri publication which appeared about 1544 to 1577 is discussed by Christian Hülsen, *Das Speculum Romanae magnificentiae des Antonio Lafreri* (1921), p. 59. See the Sales Catalogue by Barnard Quaritch (London, 1923), p. 18.

[6] Fig. 3 is from an engraving by Marco Dente in the Metropolitan Museum of Art, Print Room. Bartsch, *Le Peintre Graveur*, XIV, 195, No. 243. Passavant, *Le Peintre-Graveur*, VI, 70, No. 47. Also in Lafreri, *op. cit.*, engraving on Folio 50. Not in Hülsen. See Quaritch, *op. cit.*, p. 19, No. 197. The variation is inspired by Virgil, *Aeneid* II, 199 ff., and by a miniature in the Virgil codex Vaticanus No. 1835. See also H. Thode, *op. cit.*, p. 38, No. 66, Pl. VI.

wildest despair, while the sons are absolutely broken and helpless. The muscles are exaggerated; the hair is a wild entangled mass.

Jean de Gourmont, who worked in Paris in 1581, in a rare etching set the group on a terrace before a columned hall next to a flaming altar. Churches, the ruins of the Colosseum, a lighthouse are in the background; behind them are visible waves of the sea, a city view and distant hills (fig. 4).[6a] The figures are reversed. The older son already has both arms free and moves away. The younger son is dead and lying with the head lower than the feet.

The enthusiasm of the beginning Baroque period was partly due to the brilliant rendering of the muscles of the body, which then was the object of intensive study by Michelangelo and his contemporaries. Bandinelli, therefore, in the marble copy commissioned in 1520 by Pope Leo X, now in Florence (Figure 5), intensified the muscles as well as the expression of the face in the Baroque spirit. The contrast of light and shade could be brought out still sharper in bronze. Such a bronze model was commissioned by Bramante Lazzari (Donato d'Angelo) before his death in 1514 from Jacopo Sansovino and finished before 1523, when it was given to the Senate in Venice, from which it passed later to the Cardinal of Lorraine. Other bronze casts are in Florence (Figures 6–8), another by François Girardon was in Paris, where it was bought by Sir Robert Walpole. He put it up in his house, Houghton Hall, built in 1722–1735.[7]

[6a] I owe the illustration to the kindness of Julius Held.

[7] Manuscript of Horace Walpole, "Aedes Walpolianae; or, A Description of the Collection of Pictures at Houghton Hall in Norfolk, the Seat of Sir Robert Walpole" (1743), now in the Metropolitan Museum of Art, printed in 1747 and reprinted with additions in 1752, p. 74. If the Girardon mentioned here as the sculptor is the well-known François Girardon, the Laocoon at Houghton Hall should be added to the list of his works. An impression of the engraving by Perret, dated at Rome in 1581, is inserted in the manuscript but not in the printed editions.

The contrasts of light and shade distributed over the whole group and the strong movement are still more emphasized in the seventeenth century. The etchings by Sisto Badalocchio (1606) and by Perrier (1638)[8] depart also from the front view and thus can show interesting overlapping forms and interrupted lines. Jan Episcopius (Jan de Bisschop) ca. 1669 made two etchings of the group in which the strong Baroque character is still more stressed.[8a] Joachim von Sandrart (1616–88) drew Laocoon alone, perhaps from a small bronze cast, with right arm added and exaggerated muscles, and Gérard Audran (1640–1703) drew him in four different views and added exact measurements of the single muscles and parts of the body as a model for rules on the proportions of the human body.[9] The text to the drawings says: "The statue of Laocoon has always been considered by the most outstanding draftsmen to be wonderful, so that most have not hesitated to give it the first place among all antiquities."

The pathos of the Laocoon and the pathos of the emotional period in which the artists lived were a unity for them.

[8] Audran's drawings were first published in his *Proportions du corps humain mesurées sur les plus belles figures de l'antiquité* (1683). This treatise was first translated as: "Des menschlichen Leibes Proportionen, von denen vortrefflichsten und allerschönsten Antichen genommen und mit Fleiss abgemessen durch Mr. Audran, Professeur der Königlichen Mahler-Academie zu Paris," published by the heirs of J. J. Sandrart in Nürnberg (probably after the death of Sandrart, in 1688) with Plates 1–4 and 24–25 relating to the Laocoon. The translation in Volkmann's edition of the Teutsche Academie IV², pp. 119–130, is entitled: "Von den Verhältnissen des menschlichen Körpers nach den berühmtesten anticken Statuen abgemessen."

[8a] Jan Episcopius, *Signorum Veterum Icones*, pls. 16–17. I owe the reference to Julius Held.

[9] Joachim von Sandrart, *Teutsche Academie der Bau-Bildhauer-und Malerkunst*, I (1675, Part 2), 35; II (1679, Part 3), 88. *Sculpturae veteres admiranda* (1680), p. 4, Pl. C. *Teutsche Academie*, ed. by J. Volkmann (1771), Vol. IV, Part 2, I, 1, p. 18, Pl. C. Added are four supplementary plates by Gérard Audran in Vol. IV, Part 2, I, 3, at p. 130. The original edition in the Public Library, New York, mentions Laocoon alone with restored arm and a bronze copy, but does not give the plate. See Paul Kutter, *Joachim von Sandrart, eine kunsthistorische Studie* (1907), pp. 10 ff., 59 f., note 47.

The best proof for this is given in the fact that Titian in his altar piece of the Resurrection in SS. Nazaro e Celso at Brescia[10] has copied his Christ from the Laocoon, of which he had acquired a cast in the same year, 1522, in which he painted the altar, while for the St. Sebastian he imitated the chained slave by Michelangelo. Later Titian, however, turned away from the unlimited enthusiasm and admiration of the group. The caricature of it, which has come down to us in the woodcut by Nicolò Baldrini (Figure 9)[11] may be still more a caricature of Baccio Bandinelli's exaggerated copy and of the too great stress laid by his contemporaries on muscles and the cult of anatomy.

Domenico Theotocopuli (1548–1618), surnamed El Greco because he was born in Crete, became as a young man (1569–1570) a pupil of the old Titian in Venice. He settled in Toledo in 1576 and remained there until his death. The death of Laocoon and his sons (Figure 10) was painted around 1610 in El Greco's old age.[12] It is his only pagan motif, which he painted several times, but only the painting which came with the Kress collection in 1945 to Washington has been preserved. The movements of all three figures are more violent than in the ancient group. Laocoon as well as the younger son are already fallen backward with the legs bent and drawn

[10] Hans Tietze, *Titian Paintings and Drawings*, 1937, Pls. 55, 58–59.

[11] Fig. 9 is from the woodcut in the Metropolitan Museum, Print Room. J. D. Passavant, *Le Peintre-Graveur*, VI, 243, No. 97. Fritz Wichert, *loc. cit.*, pp. 38, 100. Hans Tietze, *op. cit.*, Fig. 327. O. Fischel, in *Amtliche Berichte der Berliner Museen*, XXXIX (1917), 59 f. H. W. Jansen, *Apes and Ape Lore in the Middle Ages and the Renaissance*, Appendix, pp. 355–368, Pl. LVI. Jansen believes that the Laocoon by Titian caricatures the controversy of his time over whether the Greek physician of Marcus Aurelius, Galen of Pergamon, used apes instead of humans for his study of anatomy.

[12] I owe the photograph for Fig. 10 to the courtesy of the Washington National Gallery, *Cat. no.* 127. August Meyer, *El Greco*, Munich, 1911. H. Kehrer, *Die Kunst des Greco*, Munich, sec. ed. 1920. Harold E. Wethep, *El Greco and His School*, Princeton, 1962, I, 50 f., 61, 63, figs. 144–145, II, 83 f.

up as in the spasm of death. The older son is still standing, but will also be killed by the snake whose head just strikes his hip. The father, in contrast, is not bitten there, but in the head as in Titian (Figure 9). In order to balance the standing son, El Greco introduced Apollo and Artemis. This pair, however, was changed by El Greco himself and defaced by later overpainting. As it appears now after cleaning the modern parts which also included loin cloths, we see three heads, two of them female, two male bodies and five legs. Probably the old El Greco wanted to keep only Apollo. In the background is the city of Toledo, which appears in many pictures by El Greco. The Trojan horse is turned to the gate of Toledo, not of Troy. There is no doubt that El Greco has surpassed the horror which emanates from the ancient group. He has been named a mannerist and has been claimed as a forerunner of Velasquez, of modern impressionism as well as of expressionism. He is, however, unique in the expression of his own artistic intentions, which agree with his own Baroque age. His painting is probably the most important one influenced by the ancient Laocoon group.

Peter Paul Rubens made about 15 drawings of the Laocoon when he saw it in Rome, 1602–1603 and 1605–1608. He drew the full group as well as many details. He seems to have been particularly fascinated by the muscular body of the father whom he drew from all sides with a particularly excellent view from the back (fig. 11), and by the younger son, whom he sketched seen from the front (fig. 12) and the back.[12a] Rubens has caught the desperate convulsions of the father and the hopeless resignation of the younger son, as well as the excitement and agitation of the violent action. He has even surpassed the pathos expressed by the Rhodian artists.

[12a] Giorgio Fubini and Julius S. Held, "Padri Rerta's Rubens Drawings after Ancient Sculpture," *Master Drawings*, Vol. 2, no. 2, 1964, pp. 123–141, Figs. 4, 6, 8, 9; pls. 1–4. I owe figs. 11–12 to the kindness of Professor Held.

His figures are as Julius Held has well said, "Less heroic in the grand manner but more human than their models. Their plight is more touching, because they are less idealized."[12b]

While the admiration for the Laocoon group persisted, the conception of the group as an example of unrestrained Baroque pathos changed in the eighteenth century through the influence of three great German classical writers, Winckelmann, Lessing, and Goethe. The classicist Winckelmann says in his first work, *Reflections on the Imitation of Greek Works in Painting and Sculpture* (1754):[13] "As the depth of the ocean remains quiet at all times, even though the surface may rage as much as possible, thus the expression of the figures of the Greeks shows a great and composed soul despite all passions. This soul describes itself in the features of Laocoon [Figures 13–14]—and not only in his features—despite the most violent suffering. One almost believes that by observing the painfully indrawn abdomen alone it is possible to experience the pain which demonstrates itself in all the sinews and muscles of the body, without glancing at the face and the other parts. Yet, this pain does not reveal itself with any fury either in the face or in the entire position. The Laocoon of the statue does not 'intone a fearful shout,' as Virgil (ii. 199 ff.) sings of his Laocoon. The opening of the mouth does not allow it; it is rather an anxious and oppressed groan. The pain of the body and the greatness of the soul are distributed and, so to speak, balanced throughout the entire frame of the figure with equal strength. Laocoon suf-

[12b] Held, *op. cit.*, p. 134.

[13] Written 1754 in Dresden, appeared there 1755 as *Gedanken über die Nachahmung der griechischen Werke in der Malerei und Bildhauerkunst.* Translated by Henry Russel as *Reflections on the Painting and Sculpture of the Greeks* (London, 1765), pp. 30 ff. The translations in the text are my own. Reprinted in the standard edition (Donaueschingen, 1825), I, 7 ff. On the Laocoon see pp. 30–33. See Carl Justi, *Winckelmann und seine Zeitgenossen,* I (1872), 382 ff.; 2d ed. (1898), pp. 351 ff.

fers, but he suffers like the Philoctetes of Sophocles. His misery touches our soul, but we would wish to be able to bear misery like this great man.

"The expression of such a great soul goes far beyond what beautiful Nature can accomplish. The artist had to feel in himself the power of the spirit which he impressed into his marble. Greece had artists and philosophers in one person. Wisdom joined hands with art, and it imbued its figures with more than common souls.

"Under a cloth, which the artists ought to have given to Laocoon as a priest, his pain would have been only half as sensible. Bernini even believed that he could discover the beginning of the effect of the poison of the snake in the thigh of Laocoon by the stiffening.

"The quieter the stance of a body is, the more apt is it to describe the true character of the soul: in all situations which deviate too much from the stance of repose the soul is not in its proper, but in a violent and forced condition. The soul becomes more easily recognizable and more significant in violent passions; it is great and noble, however, in the position of unity and of repose. The artist, in order to unite the character and the nobility of soul in one, gave to Laocoon an action which was close to the situation of repose despite such pain. But in this repose the soul has to be designated through traits which are proper to it and no other soul, in order to show it quiet, but at the same time effective, and composed, but not indifferent or sleepy."

The *History of Art* by Winckelmann (1764)[14] appeared while Lessing was still working on his *Laokoon*. Winckel-

---

[14] *Geschichte der Kunst des Altertums*, written in Rome, 1756–61, appeared 1764 in Dresden in 2 vols. Rewritten in 1763–68. Reprinted in the standard edition (Donaueschingen, 1825), Vols. III–VI. On the Laocoon see bad translation by Henry Lodge, *The History of Ancient Art* (1872). The translations in the text are my own. See Carl Justi, *op. cit.*, II (1872), 56 ff.; 2d ed., II (1898), 54 ff.; III (1872), 97 ff.; III, 2d ed. (1898), pp. 88 ff.

21

mann expanded his concept that the struggle between bodily pain and spiritual strength comprises the leading feature of our group as follows:

"Laocoon is a depiction of the most acute pain, which affects here all muscles, nerves, and veins. All parts of the body are expressed as suffering and tense, by means of which the artist has made visible all the moving springs of nature and has shown his high knowledge and art. In the presentation of this extreme suffering, however, appears the tested spirit of a great man who wrestles with necessity and wishes to check and suppress the outbreak of his emotions."

Lessing generally agreed with Winckelmann. Although he had less artistic sense, vision, and enthusiasm than Winckelmann, yet he saw more critically and clearly and possessed in addition a stronger feeling for style. Above all, he rejected the uniform treatment of the figurative arts and literature which until then had reigned unlimited and which had led Winckelmann unwittingly to equate the Laocoon group with the Philoctetes of Sophocles. Lessing pointed to the fact that in Sophocles, as in Virgil and Homer, the heroes shout and lament without being regarded as unmanly for this reason. Greatness of soul cannot therefore have been the reason that prevented the artists of our group from imitating the screaming of the Laocoon of Virgil, whose description Lessing anachronistically regarded as preceding and therefore possibly being the model for the artists of the group. According to Lessing it is beauty, the highest law of the figurative and pictorial arts that constitutes the preventive reason which here forbids disfiguration, both of the face, through ugly distortion, and of the body, through violent positions dictated by passion. Accordingly, the artists of the Laocoon softened screaming to moaning "not because crying betrays an ignoble soul, but because it disgustingly disfigures the face [Frontispiece and Figures 13–14]. Try to tear open the mouth of

Laocoon in imagination, and judge for yourself! In sculpture a merely wide opening of the mouth is a hollow that produces the most repulsive effect in the world."

Lessing thus replaces the moral reason with a formal one. At the same time, generally he is of the opinion that pictorial art, in contrast to poetry, does not have as its content truth and expression, but beauty. Its creations are destined to be repeatedly considered for a long time. Therefore, the only moment which it can grasp, in contrast to literature, must be as pregnant as possible, that is, one which leaves free play for the exercise of the imagination. Consequently, one ought not to choose, in the space arts (pictorial arts), the climactic moment of the narrative which, in the Laocoon story, would be the crying out aloud, but rather the sighing when the snake bites, for then we are much more fully able to visualize the preceding calm and succeeding cry. In contrast to this, poetry can let Laocoon cry out, for its nature as a time art enables the poet previously to acquaint us with Laocoon as a cautious patriot and loving father.

According to Lessing, then, the artists of the Laocoon have chosen the most pregnant moment, the one from which both the preceding and following stages become most comprehensible. Lessing's thesis is that figurative art postulates unity in time and must therefore confine itself within the boundaries of beauty. This theory would make the rendering of movement, action, truth, and character forever inaccessible to figurative art in contrast to poetry. This thesis, by the way, is refuted by the entire art of the Greeks.

The main emphasis of Lessing's investigation is upon poetry, which he estimates more highly and to which he assigns a much larger field than to pictorial or figurative arts. His characterization of this group as a sculptural illustration from Virgil clearly exemplifies this. Deviations are, again, explained from the law of beauty. The difference in the appearance of Laocoon—in Virgil, full priestly robe; in the group, naked—Lessing explains away "because a garment being the work of slave hands has less beauty than the work of eternal wisdom, an organized body." Lessing similarly disentangles the disparity in the ensnaring by the snakes. Virgil describes the snakes as coiling first around the boys. It is only after the arrival of their father that these snakes commence to encircle him. This they do in a double manner, around both neck and body, and then tower high above him with their heads. In contrast to this temporal development, in the group both father and sons are bound together in one knot.

Lessing had before his eyes for this description the incorrect restorations of the Vatican group (Figures 1–2).[15] An attempt by Michelangelo to replace the father's right arm (Figure 15) had already corrected the worst error.[16] An arm found by Ludwig Pollak in Rome (Figure 16)[17] proved to belong to the father, and with its help Magi could correct the general outline of the group (Figures 19, 20, 30–32). A good restoration using this arm had already been made in a cast by Georg Treu in Dresden (Fig. 17).[18] The snake, which

[15] The most important restorations were: Laocoon, whole right arm with shoulder and snake, part of the other snake near Laocoon's left knee. Elder son, tip of nose, right hand and part of arm above the snake, part and head of the snake biting into the hip of Laocoon. Younger son, right arm with uppermost coil of snake, tip of nose. See the exact list of restorations in Walter Amelung, *Sculpt. Vat. Mus.*, II, 181–84, and Werner Fuchs in Helbig, Führer, 4 ed. Speier, I, p. 162 f.

[16] Camille Sittl, *Empirische Studien über die Laokoongruppe* (1895), p. 15, Pl. III, Fig. 4; Richard Föster, in *Jahrbuch des deutschen archäologischen Instituts* (i.e., *Arch. Jahrb.*), XXI (1906), 5; Amelung, *loc. cit.*, pp. 201, 205, No. 74b.

[17] Ludwig Pollak, in *Römische Mitteilungen*, XX (1905), 277–82, Pl. VIII; Amelung, *loc. cit.*, pp. 195, 205, No. 74a.

[18] Dresden, Museum of Casts in the Albertinum, reconstruction by Georg Treu. M. Pohlenz in *Die Antike*, IX (1933), 57, Fig. 1. M. Bieber, *The Sculpture of the Hellenistic Age*, p. 134, Fig. 530. For the new restoration see F. Magi, "Il repristino del Laocoonte," *Memorie Accademia Romana di Archeologia*, IX, 1960, pp. 5–59, Ills. I–L.

in the early restorations is upraised high by Laocoon's right hand, coils about the nape of his neck, and neither the arm of Laocoon nor that of the younger son was lifted as high as the earlier restorers assumed. With the correct restoration the difference between the description of Virgil and the sculptured group becomes still stronger than Lessing had supposed. The real and fundamental reason for this difference is that the group is dependent, not upon literary, but upon pictorial or figurative tradition. We can grasp one pictorial tradition in two Pompeian wall paintings copied from a Hellenistic prototype. One is lost, the other is in the recently excavated House of Menander (Figure 18).[19] Consequently Lessing's assumption that Virgil was the only one who permitted the children to be killed together with the father is erroneous, for the prototype of these two pictures as well as the sculptural group antedate Virgil. The poet indeed agrees more with the pictures than with the sculpture. In the *Aeneid* as in the wall paintings the sons are attacked and killed earlier than the father, not at the same time as in the group. In the wall painting Laocoon is also fully dressed as he is in Virgil.

Lessing saw that Winckelmann's dating in the period of Alexander the Great, which for him was part of the best period of art, is too early. On the other hand Lessing's own dating, in the principate of Titus (79–81 A.D.), is too late. Epigraphical investigation of Rhodian inscriptions seemed to have established the date 80–20 B.C. for the masters of the Laocoon.[20] Thus Hagesandros, Athenodoros, and Polydoros

[19] Fig. 18 from Amadeo Maiuri, *La Casa di Menandro,* pp. 40 f., Fig. 17, Pl. IV.

[20] Hiller von Gaertringen, in *Arch. Jahrb.,* IX (1894), 33–37. Christian Blinkenberg and Karl F. Kinch, "*Exploration archéologique de Rhodes,* Rapport III, in K. Danske Videnskabernes Selskabs Forhandlinger" (Bulletin de l'Académie royale des Sciences et des Lettres de Danemark, Copenhague), 1905, pp. 75–83; Förster, in *Arch. Jahrb.,* XXI (1906), 23–25. Blinkenberg, in *Röm. Mitt.,* XLII (1927), 177 ff.

could not have created the group later than the publication of the *Aeneid,* which did not appear before the death of Virgil in 19 B.C. The exact date of the group is probably *ca.* 50 B.C.

Such a historical attitude was completely foreign to the spirit of the third great German author to occupy himself with the Laocoon. Goethe's vision searched for the human in man and art. Therefore Goethe's viewpoint toward the Laocoon group is a general human one. In his essay *Upon the Laocoon* (1797–98)[21] Goethe excludes from the proper consideration of pictorial or figurative art all those subjects that are understandable only through historical knowledge. He sees and explains this group as a tragic idyll, for the fact that Laocoon is a priest being punished by a god interests him not at all: "A father slept next to his sons. They became encircled by snakes, and awaking, strive to tear themselves free from the living net." While Goethe venerated Winckelmann, he agreed with Lessing's conception of the most fertile moment as being the one that leaves free play to the imagination and excites the strongest psychological interest. Goethe surpasses both, however, in his insistence that a transitional moment must be selected in the depiction of which the work of figurative art seems really to move before our very eyes. "Shortly before, no part of the whole may have been in this situation, shortly afterwards, each part must be forced to leave this situation. In this way, the work of art will ever become alive again for millions of onlookers." Goethe finds this

[21] *Über Laokoon,* written 1797–98 in Weimar, first printed in *Propylaeen,* a periodical art review published by Goethe, 1798. Reprinted in the complete editions of Goethe's *Werke,* Stuttgart (1827–30), XXXVIII, 35 ff.; (1857), XXX, 308 ff.; (1858), XXIV, 223 ff.; Meyers Klassiker Ausgaben (Leipzig), XXII, 105 ff.; standard edition (Weimar, 1887–1919), XLVII, 101–17; Propylaeen edition (Munich, 1909–31), XII, 45–54. The opinions of Goethe are collected by E. Grumach, *Goethe und die Antike,* II, 547 ff., and Max Wegner, *Goethes Anschauung antiker Kunst,*[4] pp. 69 ff.

dictum perfectly realized in the Laocoon: "I might say that the group as it now stands is as a fixed lightning, or a wave turned into stone the moment it streams against the beach."

Goethe enumerates, in his essay on the Laocoon, a number of qualities which the greatest works, of necessity, must exhibit. He then finds all these in the Laocoon: "Living, highly organized nature, character, ideal grace, and beauty." These represent to Goethe order, clarity, easy conception, and symmetry. He particularly praises how the complexity of the Laocoon group becomes conceivable through symmetry; how it has repose despite violent movement, contrasts as well as gradations, all of which offer themselves partly to the senses and partly to the spirit. Despite high pathos it yet awakens an agreeable sensation, "lessening the storm of suffering and passion through grace and beauty."

Goethe clearly recognized how the conditions of the three figures were represented in the three stages with the highest wisdom: "The elder son is only entangled at his extremities. The younger son is encircled several times, with his breast especially constricted [Figures 1, 19–21]. The father, on the other hand, tries violently to free himself and his children from the coils." Goethe is here still misled by the wrong restoration. Yet, he finely perceived in the father a union of both bodily and spiritual suffering (Figures 1, 13, 14, 23), albeit admonishing against a too lively transposition of the effect which the work arouses within us back again into the work itself. Goethe says: "The suffering of Laocoon excites terror, indeed, in the highest degree, while the situation of the dying son [Figures 1, 19, 21] excites pity, and that of the elder son [Figures 1, 19, 20, 22] fear, yet at the same time hope for his escape. Hence, Laocoon exhausts his subject in so far as he represents and arouses all possible gradations of sentiment. The ages of life are also finely graded: a strong and well-built man who has just been bitten [Figures 23–24];

27

an elder son, the least entangled, who, while pushing the tail of the snake from off his foot, looks in sympathy toward his father [Figures 22, 25, 26]; and the younger son fainting and full of anguish [Figures 21, 23, 27, 30]."

Accordingly, Goethe finds all artistic conditions happily fulfilled in this work. He also proves the Winckelmann-Lessing discussion concerning the crying of Laocoon superfluous by observing that Laocoon could in no way cry aloud at this moment. When the snake puts her teeth into his haunch, Laocoon draws back at that moment and sobs convulsively (Figures 28–29). In doing this, he draws in air through his slightly opened mouth, draws in his abdomen, thus pushing up his chest, and throws his head back upon the nape of his neck (Figure 29). Placed thus, in this convulsive situation, Laocoon cannot as yet cry out, certainly not before the next moment when the tension relaxes and the indrawn air is thrust out. Insofar as the snakes paralyze and hamper the strong movement of the figures a certain repose and unity is spread over the group. The snakes leave the elder son lightly encircled, bite the father, and kill the younger son; in doing this they coil unbreakable fetters round all three (Figures 24–25).

On the relationship between Virgil (*Aeneid* ii. 199 ff.) and the group Goethe says: "One is most unjust to Virgil and poetry if one compares even for a moment the most complete masterpiece of sculptured art with the episodic treatment in the *Aeneid*. . . . The history of Laocoon here stands as a rhetorical argument, in which the exaggeration, if only useful, may well be approved."

Against the classicizing tendencies of the three celebrated German writers stands the quite different enthusiasm of Wilhelm Heinse, in his *Ardinghello; or The Blessed Islands* (1787, ch. iv). He pretends to write in the sixteenth century, and he indeed describes the Laocoon in the style of an enthusiastic contemporary of the Baroque style: "His whole body trembles and vacillates and burns swelling under the torturing killing poison, which expands like a spring. His features, with the beautiful curled beard, are absolutely Greek—one shudders with a glad woe at the fearfull fall of the superb criminal. The snakes execute the order of their commanders solemnly and naturally, grand in their kind, as earthquakes ravage the lands. The flesh is miraculously alive and beautiful; all muscles arise from the interior, like waves in the ocean during a tempest—hand and foot are in a cramp."

Thus, the same work of art was, for the sixteenth century and for Heinse, an example of the admired Baroque style; for Winckelmann, the instigation for an enthusiastic and moral investigation and description; for Lessing, the source of formal criticism and antiquarian, aesthetic explanations together with philological ramifications; and, for Goethe, the inspiration of a purely human investigation. With them the scientific concept became fertile soil for the aesthetic effect of the Laocoon. Not one of these authors, however, has had the slightest doubt but that the highest artistic worth should be ascribed to this group.

The influence the Laocoon group had was so strong that it lent itself even to symbolic explanation. Thus about 1820 William Blake engraved the Laocoon group with the title: "Jehovah and his two sons, Satan and Adam, as they were copied from the Cherubim of Solomon's Temple by three Rhodians and applied to Natural Fact or the History of Ilium." [22] This surprising statement is explained by sentences engraved about the plate, such as: "The Gods of Priam

[22] The drawing was made from a cast in the Antique School of the Royal Academy in 1815. It is reproduced in an engraving with the inscriptions in Keynes, *The Writings of William Blake*, London, III, 357–60, Pl. LVIII. The drawing alone is used as an illustration in Abraham Rees, *Cyclopaedia or Universal Dictionary of Arts, Sciences and Literature* (1820), Vol. IV of Plates, Sculpture, Pl. III. See Keynes, centenary edition: *Poetry and Prose of William Blake*, London, 1956, pp. 280–82. Archibald Russel, *The Engravings of William Blake*, London (1956), II, 49.

are the Cherubim of Moses and Solomon, The Hosts of Heaven." "Spiritual War: Israel delivered from Egypt is Art delivered from Nature and Imitation." "Art can never exist without Naked Beauty displayed." The one serpent is called by Blake "Evil" and the other "Good and Lilith" (Adam's first wife). This is the last time that the group incited a creative spirit, as it did in the sixteenth, seventeenth, and eighteenth centuries.

The pendulum swung to the opposite extreme in the middle of the nineteenth century, when the Laocoon group became the object of undeserved censure. An example of this attitude is found for the first time in Brunn, *History of the Greek Artists:*[23] "Let us confess it: Despite the enormous tension of all forms we encounter a certain meagerness and dryness in the treatment of all surface planes and their connections. The softness and the finer transitions through which nature even in violent motions does not neglect to mediate the contrasts of the single parts are lacking. We deceive ourselves in believing that we admire the artist, while it is only the virtuosity of the artist which attracts us." Thus Brunn almost excuses himself for his lack of appreciation. He quotes the artist Johann Heinrich von Dannecker as unwilling to look for a longer time at the Laocoon when another more beautiful work was set beside it.

A. S. Murray, in his much used handbook,[24] even says: "In the group of Laocoon we are again invited to sup of horrors, and this, it should be here observed, is a new departure in art. For while older sculpture never shunned deeds of extreme violence and pain, provided there was a strong and

[23] Heinrich Brunn, *Geschichte der griechischen Künstler*, Munich (1852), pp. 475 ff., 2d ed. (1889), pp. 332 ff.

[24] A. S. Murray, *A History of Greek Sculpture*, London (1883), revised edition (1890), II, 362 ff. For the changed attitude of the different periods see also the short remarks of V. Simkhovitch, "Approaches to History, V," in *Political Science Quarterly*, XLIX (1934), 55–59.

healthy reason to fall back on, here we have them executed with cool deliberation in the Farnese bull and by means of ignoble agency in the Laocoon. In both cases the fable supplies an explanation, but a work of art should, to be successful, in its principal effect be independent of all explanation that would limit it to a particular place or time. Such limitations could be indicated in secondary details even in so peculiarly local a story as that of Laocoon and his two sons. The fable justifies the combined and simultaneous punishment of father and sons, when it tells that one of the crimes of Laocoon had been his marriage. It was this version of the story which Virgil had before him. But it was not altogether this version that was used by the sculptures of the marble group . . . they seem to have taken into account the oldest version of the legend we know of, that given by Proclos as an excerpt from the Iliupersis of Arctinos of Miletos, where Laocoon and only one of his sons perish."

Soon afterwards Lucy Mitchell, in her book on ancient sculpture,[25] reaches the peak of aversion to the Laocoon: "This terrible group gives no idea as to the beginning of the calamity. . . . The colossal form of the father, towering above his sons, is disproportionately larger than theirs; and his anguish seems correspondingly great. No consciousness of their distress is evident either in his face or form, in which pain, terrible and blinding, seems to have smothered every other feeling. This we see in the aimless movements of his legs, the agony of the cramped toes, the terrible contraction and writhing of the loins, the blind grasping at the serpent's neck with the left hand [Figure 25], and the tortured expression of the face. . . . In vain do we look here for an heroic struggling with destiny, such as Lessing imagined in the scene. . . . The only ameliorating chord in this dirge of

[25] Lucy M. Mitchell, *A History of Ancient Sculpture*, II, New York (1888), 601 ff.

agony is the sympathetic look of the elder son up to his father [Figure 26] and the hope he may have for his possible escape. . . . It is only when we study the skillful anatomy, the pyramidal grouping, and masterly technique of the Laocoon trio that we are in some degree reconciled to the revolting scene."

Nonetheless, Ernest Arthur Gardner, in his handbook [26] denounces the Laocoon "as the last and most extreme example of Pergamene art, which strives after exaggerated pathos by an actual representation of pain and agony, and refuses no device that may add to the dramatic, almost theatrical, effect, because such a device does not readily harmonize with the principles of sculpture . . . however much we may admire the skill with which he has rendered his repulsive subject, the choice of such a subject in itself suffices to show that he —or rather the age in which he lived—had lost the finer instinct for sculptural fitness. . . . Such pathological study . . . would be justified . . . if its realism was equalled by its correctness. But one cannot help feeling that the motive for the whole is inadequately rendered. The snakes have no truth to nature, but are zoological monstrosities . . . one of them is biting like a dog." The head of the snake is restored! (See Figures 22–24.)

The old admiration, however, persisted in France in the nineteenth century. Hippolyte Taine [27] calls the art of the Laocoon "new, sentimental, expressive. It shows itself in the terrible and touching character of the subject, in the atrocious reality of the undulating bodies of the serpents, in the afflicting weakness of the poor little boy who is to die presently [Figure 23], in the finish of the muscles, of the torso, and of

[26] Ernest Arthur Gardner, *A Handbook of Greek Sculpture* (1896–97; revised edition 1911), pp. 469 ff.

[27] Hippolyte Taine, *Voyage en Italie*, I (12th ed., Rome, 1905), 156. It was written in 1864.

the foot [Figure 35], in the painful inflation of the veins, and in the subtle anatomy of suffering."

Louis Viardot[28] in his *Merveilles de la sculpture* says, "The Laocoon resists better the terrifying proof of a first look. All imitations and copies, even the one of which Bandinelli was so proud [Figure 5], are so far below the original that one is surprised and delighted to discover in it from the beginning unexpected beauties. One understands the opinion of Pliny among the ancients and of Michelangelo, Lessing, and Diderot among the moderns, who all give the palm to this celebrated group. One understands the festival which the Romans celebrated in honor of its discovery on June 1, 1506, under Pope Julius II. The Laocoon is not surpassed by any other piece of sculpture in the expression of physical pain, and in the will power stronger than pain . . ."

Today, we can again be just to the Laocoon group without falling into the exaggerated admiration of the sixteenth, seventeenth, and eighteenth centuries. We can now judge the group historically as a late example of Hellenistic Baroque in a period already transitional to the classicizing tendencies of the late Republican and Augustan era. That it appears as more intensely Baroque to us than it did to the authors of the seventeenth and eighteenth centuries is due to their being literally surrounded with such exaggerated examples of Baroque painting, drawing, and sculpture (Figures 2–12), so that the Laocoon appeared as temperate in comparison. The most instructive analogy in this regard is to be had by comparing the Laocoon of Bandinelli in marble (Figure 5), other examples of adaptations in bronze (Figures 6–8), and engravings (Figures 2–4) of the sixteenth century with the Hellenistic group.

More recent descriptions give clear accounts of the

---

[28] Louis Viardot, *Merveilles de la sculpture* (1869), p. 129.

actual subject. An excellent example is that of Amelung:[29] "We see an action full of terror. An elderly bearded man and two boys are surrounded by two enormous snakes. The smaller of the boys is already writhing in the most intense pain, for the teeth of one of the snakes have perforated his side. The man vainly strives to evade the snake by bending sidewise and to tear the snake away from his hip, in which he already feels the beginning of the bite [Figures 19–24]. Hope of escape seems to exist for the older boy alone [Figures 25–26, 30–32]. Yet he also has been firmly entangled and pity for the man who is wrestling so agonizedly and toward whom the dying glance of the smaller boy is also directed paralyzes him, freezing him to his place. No help! The godhead of the altar, upon which the man has sunk back, feels no pity. We suspect that a punishing judgment, sent and willed by a god, is being executed here. As the man had a laurel wreath, he must have been a priest of Apollo. Wreath and altar bring us into the interior of a sacred precinct, where the priest, ministered to by the two boys, had prepared a sacrifice. All three stood turned to the altar. They hear the rustling and whistling of the snakes coupled with the shouts of the horror-stricken people. Terrified, they turn around, but are not given even one moment for deliberation. One of the snakes, beginning from the right, coils around all three. The other has chosen, as her victim, the father, whom she attacks from the left and behind. Two of the unfortunates are destined to die with the speed of lightning. For the third alone there remains a torturing and fearful uncertainty."

Against this deeply felt narrative description of the action may be set the purely aesthetic analyses—disregarding the content of the group—of Krahmer[30] and the following of Valentin Müller:[31]

[29] Amelung, *Skulpturen des Vatikanischen Museums* II, 184 ff. The translation is by this author.

"It is very fortunate that we possess a monument dated within the following, last phase and displaying the very characteristics which we are compelled to postulate for it according to the cyclical development which we are trying to discover. A better checking up could not be found. The monument referred to is the Laokoon group, generally dated about 50 B.C. on account of the lifetime of the sculptors. The balance is again broken up, and intensified movement is given. Diagonal lines prevail, not vertical and horizontal ones. Dissolution and detail have gone as far as was possible in Greek art. This is especially clear in Laokoon's head. The composition is most complicated, showing an incessant interruption and contrasting of lines. It is a jumping from spot to spot. Following the contour we have as accents: right foot of the younger son, garment, right buttock, left arm, snake's coil, right arm, Laokoon's elbow, his head, left upper arm, right hand of elder son, his shoulder, his head, garment, knee, snake's coil, garment. The result is a choppy rhythm in spite of the incessant movement, not an imposing and full swing.

"A comparison between the head of the Laokoon and one of the giants from the Pergamene altar done in the *maniera grande* of the balanced stage is very instructive. The curls of Laokoon's beard look crumpled. There is something inorganic in them which reminds one of the manner in which hair and beard are rendered in the portrait of Poseidonios. A similarity in the structure of the forms is, indeed, apparent in the two heads, if we account for the differences due to the difference in phase. The Poseidonios has the solidity and restraint of the initial phase, the Laokoon the dissolution and intensification of the closing phase.

---

[30] Gerhard Krahmer, "Die einansichtige Gruppe und die späthellenistische Kunst," in *Nachrichten der Göttinger Gesellschaft der Wissenschaften*, Philologisch-Historische Klasse (1927), pp. 53 ff., Figs. 1–2.

[31] Valentin Müller, in *Art Bulletin* (1938), pp. 410 ff.

"Few archeologists will deny that the Laokoon means an end. It seems as though the development could not be pushed farther. The dissolution and attention to detail has reached the extreme point. Furthermore we have the impression that the creative power has also come to an end. To be sure, the Laokoon as well as the Homer are still remarkable works, but compared to the earlier ones they show an inner barrenness. They are like ghosts, an outer mask only, without inner life and substance. It is the last flaring of the flame before it dies down.

"Now the phase to which the Laokoon belongs proves by its position in the cycle of development that it must be a terminating one. Since we found tripartition the rule, the third phase of the third stage of the third period must be the last one. With it the Hellenistic epoch is complete.

"The Laokoon clearly has a tectonic framework of lines. The body of the father in the center dominates the structure, the arms and the snakes are side lines."

The new detailed photographs by Ernest Nash bring out the high artistic and technical qualities of this masterpiece for the first time. They bring out particularly well the heads (Figures 13, 14, 26, 29, 33–34) and details such as the different character of the feet: the strength of the feet of the father (Figures 35–36); the softness in those of the elder son (Figure 38); and the cramped position of the feet of the younger son (Figure 37), as well as the weakness of his hand, vainly striving to push away the snake that bites into his flank (Figures 21, 27).

The descriptions of the classical writers evince a feeling which perhaps only now we can fully appreciate with these new photographs before us. We have just begun to value the Hellenistic Greek art as well as the Baroque art of the sixteenth century more justly than the nineteenth century has done. Thus Pohlenz[32] has recently rightly compared the Laocoon in its importance for art to the importance of the Stoic philosophy as developed by Panaitios of Rhodes, the compatriot of the artists. Just as Panaitios's manly humanity has been adopted by Cicero, whose philosophy was so important for the Romans, thus the manly suffering of pain represented so perfectly in this group by the contemporaries of Cicero has influenced Roman art. We moderns, however, with our analytical criticism, are likely to lose the feeling for the essential which the artists and the writers of the sixteenth–eighteenth centuries had. We therefore can still learn much today from them for the appreciation and enjoyment of art.

The new finds of Jacopi in the cave belonging to a villa of Tiberius at Sperlonga near Gaeta[33] have freed the Laocoon from its isolation, but they have not changed its unique value. The first impression that the cave had yielded a replica of the Laocoon was due to the fact that similar snakes coiled about human bodies. These snakes, however, are the legs of Scylla, ending in the heads of dogs and fishes, who attack the companions of Odysseus. Under his ship is a plaque with the names of the three artists who, according to Pliny, worked on the Laocoon. In this case the names of their fathers are added: Athanodoros, son of Agesandros; Agesandros, son of Paionios; Polydoros, son of Polidoros, from Rhodes. The three artists thus are not related to each other, but they come from long established Rhodian workshops.[34] As the inscription is added in the first century A.D. according to the authority on

[32] Max Pohlenz, "Laokoon," in *Antike*, IX (1933), 54 ff.

[33] Giulio Jacopi, *L'antro di Tiberio a Sperlonga,* Instituto di Studi Romani Editore, I Monumenti Romani, IV, 1963. Idem, *L'Antro di Tiberio e il Museo Archeologico Nazionale di Sperlonga.* Itenerari dei Musei Gallerie e Monumenti d'Italia, Instituto poligrafico dello Stato, Roma 1965.

[34] Gisela M. A. Richter, *Three Critical Periods in Greek Sculpture,* Oxford, 1951, pp. 66–70.

epigraphy, Margherita Guarducci,[35] they cannot tell us any-thing about the original date. It seems that the inscription replaced an earlier one on the base, just as the altar on which Laocoon sinks is a later Roman addition in marble from Luna instead of the Greek marble used for the figures. It may have been originally used also for the altar, when the group was created in Rhodes.

These and other important discoveries we owe to the painstaking work of Filippo Magi.[36] He has taken the group apart and reconstructed it again under sharp observation of all details. The work took three years. The results are aston-ishing, and we now possess a much better and more valuable group. We can trust that we now see it as the three artists, after careful planning, had created it (Figures 19–20, 30–32). The first discovery of Magi was that the arm found by Pollak (Figure 16) belongs to the Vatican group, not to a copy. The second was that the group was not carved from one block but in eight pieces. The surfaces of the parts where they joined each other are undulated and so well worked that the joints fit exactly into one another without dowels. Indeed it looks as if the group were in one piece. This is one of the reasons that careful planning (*consilii sententia*) of the three artists was necessary. The brilliant technique shows a long workshop tradition inherited from father to son through all the Hellenistic periods. The Baroque style of which the Laocoon is the culmination lasted longer in Rhodes than in Pergamon.

Another important discovery of Magi is the fact that the right foot of the older son was farther away from the

[35] Margherita Guarducci, "Iscrizione imprecatoria da Sperlonga," *Rendi-conti dell' Accademia Nazionale dei Lincei,* Classe di Scienze Morali, Storia e Filosofia, Serie VIII, Vol. XV, 1960, pp. 5–7.

[36] Filippo Magi, "Il Ripristino del Laocoonte," *Memorie della Pontificia Accademia Romana di Archeologia,* Serie III, vol. IX, 1960, pp. 5–59, pls. I–L.

left foot of Laocoon than in the first restoration (Figure 1). This moves him a little more to the outside and away from the place of disaster. His final escape thus becomes clearer than before (Figure 19).

The new restoration of the full laurel wreath due to the priest of Apollo makes the head of Laocoon still more prominent than before as the apex of the group (Figure 20). It is above the diagonal line which goes through the shoulders and arms of father and elder son to the pointed elbow of Laocoon. The head of the older son is only half above this diagonal line. A second diagonal line runs parallel to the upper one extending from the left foot and right knee of the older son and the snake coiling from the ankle of the older to the shoulders of the younger son. The right arm of the younger son is restored, probably rightly, similarly to the right arm of Laocoon. The bent arms correct the wrong pull upwards of the first reconstruction and replace it with a pull backward toward the altar on which Laocoon has sacrificed.

Despite the bent arms the contour of the whole group now seems more closed than before. It remains a onesided group in which we can observe all important actions in one glance, if we take a moderate distance. Thus, the actions of all hands can be seen better than before. All three right hands make ineffective gestures. The father puts his hand behind his head, the younger son on his head. The older son makes a gesture of despair and sympathy. The left hands, in contrast, are all active, but to no avail. Laocoon tries to remove the neck of the snake, whose head has already struck his hip. The younger son does the same to the head of the lower snake at his right side, but is already dying. Only the older son will easily strip the coil of the same snake from his left leg, again emphasizing his escape.

Thus, all main motifs are clear in the front. Yet, side view (Figure 30) and back views (Figures 31–32) are also necessary, particularly to grasp the complicated movements of the two snakes. It is fortunate that Magi has removed the group from the wall so that one can study the back. There is considerable depth used by the Rhodian artists, in contrast to Greek classical groups.

The date of the Laocoon group was almost unanimously accepted as about 50 B.C., established by Blinkenberg.[37] The distinguished scholar Gisela Richter tried to give it a date around 150, near or shortly after the Pergamon altar,[38] while Magi and Howard preferred a date before this Baroque masterpiece.[39] Other scholars believe the first date to be still the right one, thus Sichterman and this author.[40]

We must, however, wait for the final reconstruction and dating of the other Homeric groups from Sperlonga before we can definitely date the Laocoon. This author has no doubt that the Laocoon is much nearer to the Scylla and Polyphemus groups than to the Pergamon altar. The head of Laocoon is related to the head of Odysseus (Jacopi, Figure 29, and Figures 85–86). The body of Laocoon has bulging muscles similar to those of several torsos in Sperlonga (Figures 20, 79–83, 90). The bodies and coils of the snakes are also similar. For the composition we must wait for a good reconstruction of the Sperlonga groups, which has not yet been achieved. In any case the Sperlonga groups are near in

[37] Blinkenberg, *Röm. Mitt.* XX, 1905, pp. 277 ff.

[38] See Gisela M. A. Richter, *op. cit.*, Figs. 66–72.

[39] Magi, *op. cit.*, pp. 39–46. Seymour Howard, "Another Prototype for the Gigantomachy of Pergamon," *AJA*, 68, 1964, pp. 129–136, pls. 39–40.

[40] Giulio Jacopi, "Gli Autori del Laocoonte e la loro cronologia," *Archeologia Classica* X, Rome 1958, pp. 160–163. Margarete Bieber, *The Sculpture of the Hellenistic Age*, revised ed., N.Y., 1961, p. 134 f. Hellmut Sichtermann, *Laokoon*, Opus Nobile 3, Meisterwerke der antiken Kunst, Bremen 1957; idem "Der wiederhergestellte Laokoon," *Gymnasium* 70, 1963, pp. 193 ff.; idem, *Laokoon*, Einführung, Stuttgart, 1964. Howard, *op. cit.*, p. 131, note 8 quotes this author as agreeing to the early date of Gisela Richter. I have, on p. 135, note 72, quoted her new date, but I have not accepted it.

subject matter and cruel mood to the Laocoon. There can be no doubt that they are works by the same Rhodian masters. The artists also needed careful planning for the complicated stories of the attack on the ship of Odysseus with Scylla's many tentacles and the blinding of Polyphemus by Odysseus and his companions. It seems to me that the Laocoon, so highly praised by Pliny after at least 130 years, when he wrote the preface to his work in 77 A.D., must be the mature masterpiece of the three Rhodians. The first half of the first century is a very plausible period for the Homeric groups in Sperlonga. At that time Rhodes was recovering from a setback by Delos and was a dependent ally of the Romans.

In any case the spirit of the groups in Sperlonga is nearer to the Laocoon than to the Pergamene Gigantomachy. When one compares them, one feels the battle as a tragedy and the frieze seems to be a full-blooded creation of great artists. The Homeric groups are terrifying spectacles, sophistically contrived with cool calculation in all the details. There are certainly elements which also occur in the Pergamon altar. In this altar of Zeus there appear classical elements and they also appear in the group. The movements of the legs of Laocoon, those of a man falling down, begin to appear in the fifth century; the figure of the younger son reminds us of the fourth century. We have indeed an eclectic work. Eclecticism and classicism are the hallmarks of the first century B.C. Greek elements of different periods are brought into a new synthesis at the end of the Hellenistic period in Greek lands as well as in the Mediterranean world, which soon became more and more Roman.

The Laocoon group is the consummation of all that the Greeks had to offer to their Roman masters. In its new form it will continue to influence artists, poets, writers, scholars, and art lovers.

LAOCOON

Fig. 1. Group of Laocoon, earlier Restoration.

The engraving shows text inscribed on the statue:

MRCVS·RAVENAS

· LAOCHOON ·

·ROMAE·IN·PALATI·O·PONT·IN·
·LOCO·QVI·VVLGO·DICITVR·
·BELVEDERE·

Fig. 2.   Engraving of the Group by Marco Dente.

Fig. 3. Engraving of the Group by Marco Dente.
Changed to conform to Virgil.

Fig. 4. Laocoon, etching by Jean de Gourmont.

Fig. 5. Laocoon Group by Bandinelli.

Fig. 6. Bronze Group of Laocoon, XVI century.

Figs. 7–8. Bronze Groups of Laocoon.

Fig. 9. Three Monkeys imitating Laocoon, after Titian's Caricature. *Woodcut by Nicolo Boldrini.*

Fig. 10. Painting by El Greco.

Fig. 11.   Drawing by Rubens, Back of Laocoon.

Fig. 12.   Drawing by Rubens, the Younger Son.

Fig. 13.   Front View of Head of Laocoon.

Fig. 14. Head of Laocoon, three quarter view.

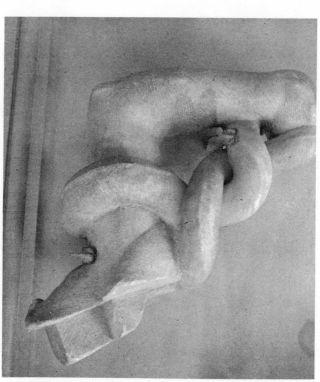

Fig. 15. Right Arm of Laocoon by Michelangelo.

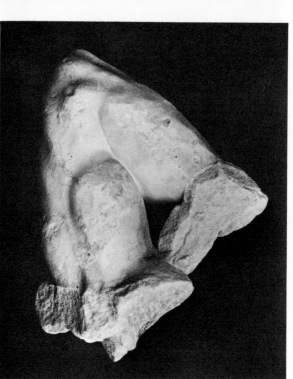

Fig. 16. Right Arm of Laocoon, found by Pollak, now used for the Group.

Fig. 17.   Reconstruction of the Group in Dresden.

Fig. 18.   Death of Laocoon and his sons,
Wallpainting in Casa di Menandro, Pompeii.

Fig. 19. Group of Laocoon and his Sons, reconstructed by Magi.

Fig. 20. Group of Laocoon and his Sons, restored by Magi.

Fig. 22. Elder Son of Laocoon.

Fig. 21. Younger Son of Laocoon.

Fig. 23. Upper Part of the Group.

Fig. 24. Lower Part of the Group.

Fig. 25.　Lower Part of the Elder Son.

Fig. 26. Upper Part of the Elder Son.

Fig. 27. Upper Part of the Younger Son.

Fig. 28. Upper Part of Laocoon.

Fig. 29. Head of Laocoon, Profile.

Fig. 30.   Side View of Group.

Fig. 31.   Back View of Group, reconstructed by Magi.

Fig. 32. Back View of Group, restored by Magi.

Fig. 33. Head of Elder Son.

Fig. 34. Head of Younger Son.

Fig. 35. Right Foot of Laocoon, Side View.

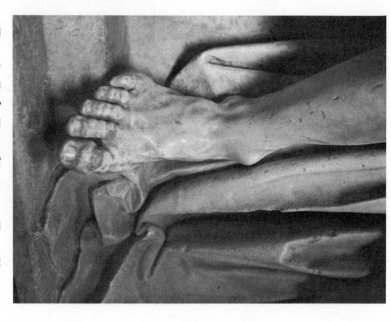

Fig. 36. Right Foot of Laocoon, Front View.

Fig. 38. Left Foot of Laocoon
and Feet of Elder Son.

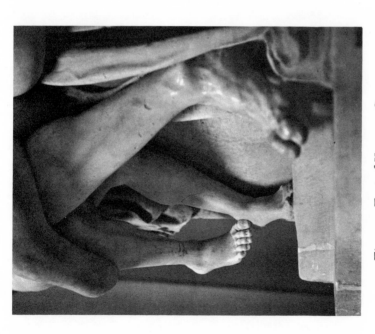

Fig. 37. Feet of Younger Son.

The manuscript was prepared for publication by Ralph Busick.
The book was designed by Joanne E. Colman and Richard Kinney.
The typeface for the text is Mergenthaler Linotype's Caledonia
designed by W. A. Dwiggins in 1937. The display face is Perpetua
designed by Eric Gill, 1929–30 for the Monotype Corporation.
The book is printed on Mead Paper Company's
Moistrite Offset paper and bound in
Columbia Mills Bayside Chambray over boards.
Manufactured in the United States of America.